Little Sharks, BIG Sharks

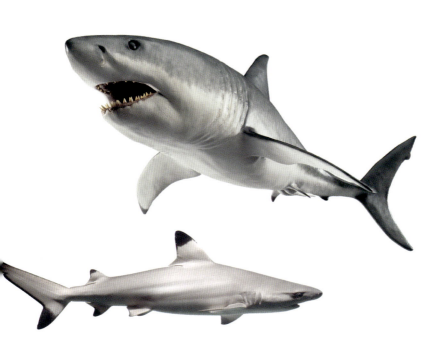

THIS EDITION
Editorial Management by Oriel Square
Produced for DK by WonderLab Group LLC
Jennifer Emmett, Erica Green, Kate Hale, *Founders*

Editors Grace Hill Smith, Libby Romero, Maya Myers, Michaela Weglinski;
Photography Editors Kelley Miller, Annette Kiesow, Nicole DiMella;
Managing Editor Rachel Houghton; **Designers** Project Design Company;
Researcher Michelle Harris; **Copy Editor** Lori Merritt; **Indexer** Connie Binder; **Proofreader** Larry Shea;
Reading Specialist Dr. Jennifer Albro; **Curriculum Specialist** Elaine Larson

---

Published in the United States by DK Publishing
1745 Broadway, 20th Floor, New York, NY 10019

Copyright © 2023 Dorling Kindersley Limited
DK, a Division of Penguin Random House LLC
23 24 25 26 10 9 8 7 6 5 4 3 2 1
001-334008-July/2023

All rights reserved.

Without limiting the rights under the copyright reserved above, no part of this publication may be reproduced, stored in or introduced into a retrieval system, or transmitted, in any form, or by any means (electronic, mechanical, photocopying, recording, or otherwise), without the prior written permission of the copyright owner.
Published in Great Britain by Dorling Kindersley Limited

A catalog record for this book
is available from the Library of Congress.
HB ISBN: 978-0-7440-7335-5
PB ISBN: 978-0-7440-7336-2

DK books are available at special discounts when purchased in bulk for sales promotions, premiums, fundraising, or educational use. For details, contact: DK Publishing Special Markets,
1745 Broadway, 20th Floor, New York, NY 10019
SpecialSales@dk.com

Printed and bound in China

The publisher would like to thank the following for their kind permission to reproduce their images:
a=above; c=center; b=below; l=left; r=right; t=top; b/g=background

Alamy Stock Photo: Biosphoto / Bruno Guenard 8br, Dan Burton Photo 28-29, Charles Hood 26-27, imageBROKER / Norbert Probst 20-21, 21bc, 21br, Louise Murray 24br, Erik Schlogl 11br; **Getty Images: I**mage Source / George Karbus Photography 27br, imageBROKER / Norbert Probst 13tc, 31clb, Moment Open / NiCK 20br, Photodisc / Jason Edwards 13bl, Staff 14br, 14-15, 15tr, 15bc, 31cla, The Image Bank / Gerard Soury 26br; **Getty Images / iStock:** atese 22-23, E+ / BartCo 23br, lindsay_imagery 30, mihtiander 24-25, USO 22ca, Velvetfish 12-13; naturepl.com: Franco Banfi 6-7b, Andy Murch 6-7, 7t, 7bc, Alex Mustard 12br; **Shutterstock.com:** Aaronejbull87 28br, AshtonEa 10-11, Craig Lambert Photography 10br, Edgar Photosapiens 4clb, Fata Morgana by Andrew Marriott 29br, Jan Finsterbusch 18-19, frantisekhojdysz 13bc, 16-17, 17bl, Dirk van der Heide 11bl, Andrea Izzotti 31cl, Izen Kai 31bl, Kletr 16br, 30br, nicolasvoisin44 31bl/1, Martin Prochazkacz 19bc, SergeUWPhoto 5tc, wildestanimal 4-5, 8-9, 9bc, 18br, 31tl, Dotted Yeti 24-25c, 25bl;

Cover images: *Front:* **Getty Images / iStock:** Pacha M Vector; **Shutterstock.com:** Maquiladora cl, cra;
Back: **Shutterstock.com:** Maquiladora (x3)

All other images © Dorling Kindersley
For more information see: www.dkimages.com

For the curious
www.dk.com

Little Sharks, BIG Sharks

Ruth A. Musgrave

Some sharks are big.
Most are little.
Many are the same size as you.
Meet some sharks from littlest to biggest.

This little shark lives deep in the sea.
It does something amazing.
It glows in the dark.

velvet belly lanternshark

You are bigger than this shark.
It hunts at night.
It eats smaller fish.
It also eats crabs.

pyjama shark

9

This shark eats animals with hard shells.
It has strong teeth.

Port Jackson shark

Find the shark.
It hides in the sand.
It waits to catch a fish.

tasseled wobbegong

13

Meet a shark that lives deep in the sea. Its big mouth has a lot of teeth.

frilled shark

Look at this shark's head.
Hold out your arms.
This shark's head is about that wide.

great hammerhead shark

A blue shark has long fins. The fins help it swim fast.

blue shark

This shark has a long tail. The tail helps it catch fish.

thresher shark

This big shark hunts big animals in the sea.

great white shark

Greenland shark

This big shark swims slowly in the deep sea. The water is very cold there.

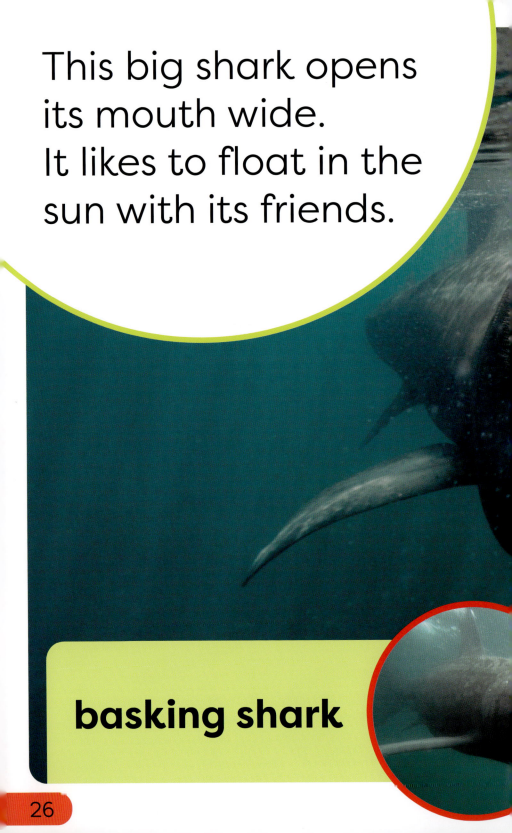

This big shark opens its mouth wide.
It likes to float in the sun with its friends.

basking shark

This is the biggest kind of shark.
Your arms are too short to give it a hug.
That is okay.

whale shark

Sharks do not like big hugs.

Little or big sharks.
Slow or fast sharks.
Sharks are a big part
of the sea.

Glossary

fin
a body part that helps a shark swim, turn, and stop

frilled shark
a shark that lives deep in the sea

great white shark
a shark that hunts seals and sea lions

tasseled wobbegong shark
a shark that hides in the sand

thresher shark
a large shark that uses its tail to hunt

Quiz

Answer the questions to see what you have learned. Check your answers with an adult.

1. What does the littlest shark do?
2. When does the pyjama shark hunt?
3. What shark has a wide head?
4. What shark floats in the sun?
5. Which shark is the biggest?

1. It glows in the dark 2. At night 3. Great hammerhead shark
4. Basking shark 5. Whale shark